JOJO SIWA

The Sweetest Dream

TRIUMPH
BOOKS

This book is available in quantity at special discounts for your group or organization. For further information, contact:

Triumph Books LLC
814 North Franklin Street
Chicago, Illinois 60610
(312) 337-0747
www.triumphbooks.com

Printed in U.S.A.

ISBN: 978-1-62937-720-9

Content written, developed, and packaged by Katy Sprinkel
Edited by Laine Morreau
Design and page production by Patricia Frey
Cover design by Preston Pisellini

Photographs by Getty Images; illustrations by iStock.

JOJO IS UNSTOPPABLE!

If you haven't heard of JoJo Siwa, then you must be living under a rock! The hugely talented fifteen-year-old burst onto the scene in 2013 as a star on the reality TV series *Abby's Ultimate Dance Competition*, and her bubbly personality and steely determination made her a fan favorite among *Dance Moms* viewers.

Known by many as JoJo with the Bow Bow—a nod to the signature hair bow that she's been wearing since she was a preschooler—she has catapulted to mega-fame as an Internet celebrity, posting regularly to her legion of Siwanatorz (her fans' chosen moniker). She has 15 million fans on Musical.ly, 8 million subscribers to her YouTube channel, 7.4 million Instagram followers, 522,000 Facebook followers, and 387,000 Twitter followers—and climbing!

But she's more than just a social media star; she's an *influencer* in the best sense of the word. JoJo takes every opportunity to use her platform for positivity. Her JoJo Bows have become a powerful statement against bullying. Her music similarly tackles the haters, encouraging fans to be themselves, be kind, and stand up for what's right.

With a slew of dance awards, a platinum single in "Boomerang," and a pair of Kids' Choice Awards, she's already getting recognition across the industry. And having signed an overall talent deal with Nickelodeon, she's already a familiar face across the network. Add to that a merchandising empire—everything from dolls to makeup to bedding (and, yes, hair bows)—and she may well be the hardest-working girl in Hollywood. One thing's for sure: the tireless JoJo shows no sign of stopping anytime soon.

SHE'S JUST
A KID AT HEART

At fifteen, she's already enjoyed a career longer than a lot of Hollywood stars. Fame can make a kid grow up fast, but JoJo pushes back against that pressure.

Watchers of *JoJo's Juice* and followers on Musical.ly don't see a scripted, choreographed, highly produced commodity. Instead, they see their idol being, well, a normal teenager—clowning around with friends, playing pranks, dancing like crazy in her own living room. She understands that people want to see the real her, and her authenticity is one of the things that resonates so deeply with her fan base.

Reflecting to Kidscreen about her popularity, she mused, "Why me? Why am I so big? It's so crazy. Maybe it's that I'm relatable, I'm a kid. I think that has to be what it is."

SHE'S A MIDWESTERN GIRL IN A HOLLYWOOD WORLD

Born May 19, 2003, Joelle Joanie Siwa spent her formative years in Omaha. And though JoJo has been in the biz since she was a little girl, the strong, midwestern values with which she was raised are still deeply rooted in her. "My parents were all about family values and making sure [my brother and I] stay[ed] grounded," she writes in *JoJo's Guide to the Sweet Life*. It's what makes her the wholesome role model that her fans know and love.

No matter how far her career has come, she still remembers where she came from. Accepting her first big award at Nickelodeon's Kids' Choice Awards, a stunned JoJo said, "I'm from Nebraska and I'm out here and I just won a Kids' Choice Award."

SHE LOVES
THE '80S!

All it takes is one look at JoJo's oversized hair bows and side ponytail—this girl loves the 1980s! JoJo seems to take all her fashion cues from the decade's fun shapes and neon brights— everything from rainbows to unicorns to sequins, sequins, sequins! "My theory is that I was actually born in the eighties and the government transplanted me to the present day. Just check the way I dress if you need proof," she quips in her autobiography, *JoJo's Guide to the Sweet Life.*

But it's not just her clothes. The singer, who threw a huge '80s-themed bash for her thirteenth birthday, puts that '80s stamp on her music too. That same playfulness is evident in her songs, which echo the upbeat mood and playful rhythms of the best '80s ladies, from Cyndi "Girls Just Want to Have Fun" Lauper to Madonna, whose iconic '80s-fabulous look was not complete without a giant hair bow.

SHE'S GOT BLING FOR HER "BOOMERANG"

JoJo's single "Boomerang" is more than just a catchy dance tune. It's an anthem for Siwanatorz, a call to arms to people everywhere to stand up to bullying—and withstand it. As of this writing, the music video, which features JoJo's real-life besties from Nebraska to L.A. and beyond, boasts more than 600 million views.

But it's far from just a viral hit. In August 2018 the single was certified platinum by the Recording Industry Association of America (RIAA), eclipsing the 1 million mark in sales. Not bad for a kid who grew up wanting to be a real-life Hannah Montana.

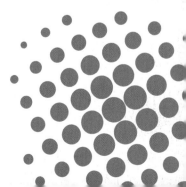

5

SHE'S ALWAYS BEEN BFFs WITH HER MOM

A lot of people assume that since Jessalynn owned a dance studio and is a former dancer herself, she thrust JoJo into the spotlight. Quite the contrary, says JoJo, who writes in her autobiography, "I was never forced to dance, or to do anything I've done over the years—but if I wanted it, my mom was right there encouraging and investing her time and energy into it." Anyone can see it, looking at them on-screen: there's a lot of love there.

And they've been in lockstep throughout JoJo's rise to fame. Her mom has been her choreographer, her teacher, her comanager, and her all-time wingwoman. It's led to a relationship far beyond mother-daughter, including being best friends. (They even have code names for each other: the respective names of their BFFs back home in Omaha: Halle and Kim.)

SHE WAS
A BABY DIVA

JoJo's love of dancing started practically at birth. She can recall being a kid, hanging out at her mom's dance studio and watching the older girls as they practiced their routines. It was an early education for a dancer, and she made the most of it.

Her first competitive dance solo came at the age of two at the Kids Artistic Revue. Still in diapers, she performed her "Baby Diva" dance routine to the song "Mama, I'm a Big Girl Now" from the musical *Hairspray*. Luckily, the Siwas were taping the performance. If JoJo felt nervous, it doesn't show. She has all the confidence and poise and sparkly rhinestone bow-ness that she possesses today. Check out https://www.youtube.com/watch?v=hrjHrbV8u3k to see the cuteness for yourself!

7

SHE EMBRACES HER INNER NERD

Learning is the bedrock of JoJo's work ethic. "In order to be really good at anything, you have to be willing to work hard and be a little different and embrace your inner nerd," she writes in her autobiography. And for a self-starter such as JoJo, homeschooling has always been the perfect fit. From an early age, it's allowed her to be more flexible with her schedule, first accommodating the demands of competitive dance and now her current and unpredictable Hollywood life.

More important, it's allowed her to apply her laser focus to subjects that interest her. It was her idea to add computer classes on video editing and recording software to her curriculum. That's no small thing when you consider that without that training, the YouTube galaxy would have been without one of its brightest stars.

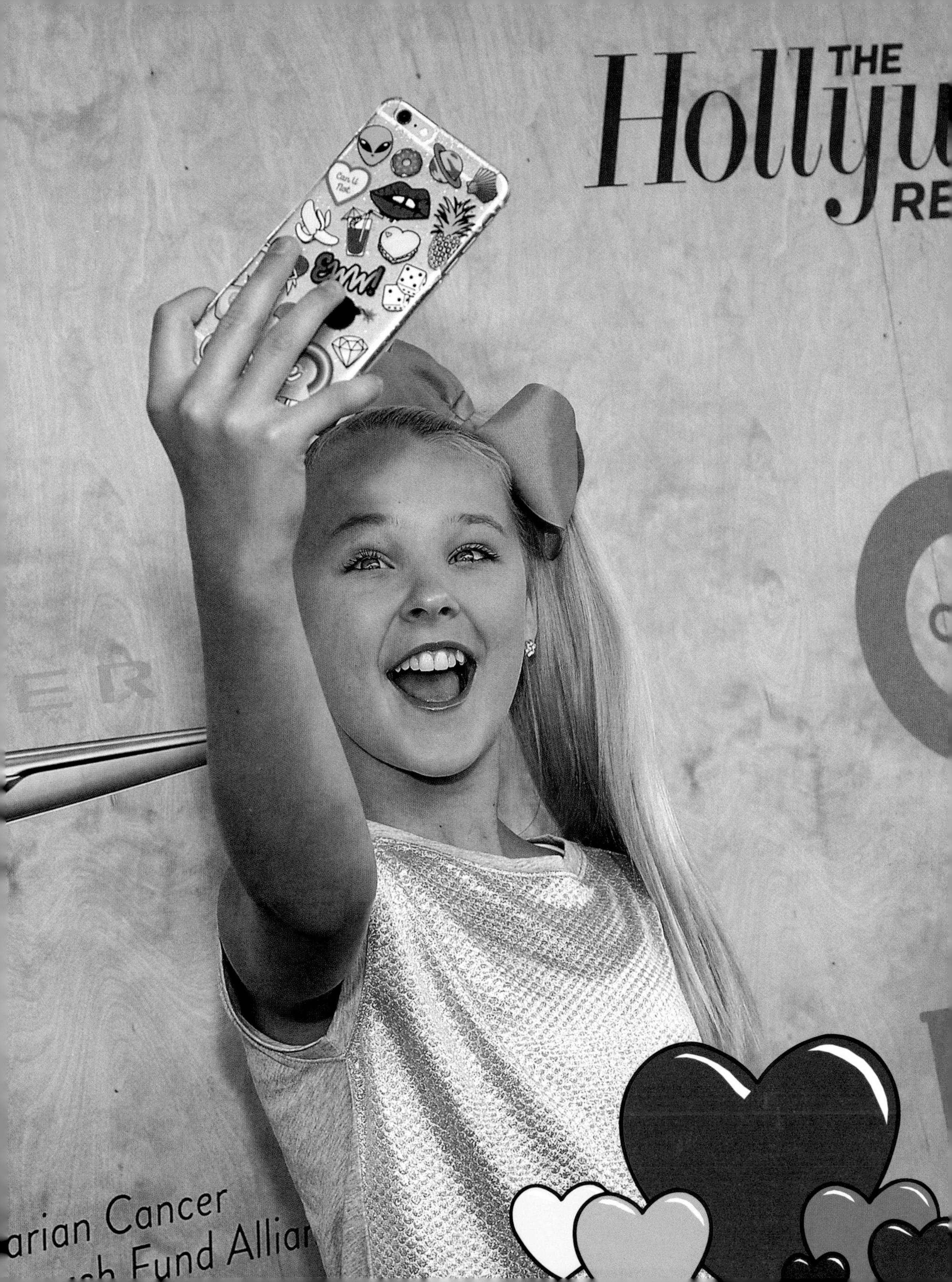
THE
Can U Not
EWW!
arian Cancer

SHE'S BEEN BULLIED TOO

Unfortunately, like everyone has or will be at some point, JoJo has endured her fair share of bullying, both in person and online. But she knows the secret to overcoming negativity. It all starts with perspective.

She vividly remembers her first encounter with Internet haters, when she was an eight-year-old reality show contestant. She was in tears, but her mom quickly brought her back to earth by accentuating the positive. Relating the story to Smart Entertainment Group, she remembered her mom's reaction. "Why would you respond to the one [comment] that's mean?" her mom asked. "Respond to the thousand that are nice and loving and caring."

From there came JoJo's three-pronged strategy for dealing with online criticism: "a) [don't] listen to it, b) listen to the happy ones, and c) delete and block," JoJo continued to SEG.

SHE'S MUSICAL.LY TALENTED

Every one of JoJo's 15 million fans on Musical.ly could tell you that she's perfectly suited for the platform. The social networking app, which launched in 2014, was created as a vehicle for users to create, cut, and upload their own music videos. Today, it's one of the most popular apps available.

JoJo's offerings range from the humorous to the sincere, and many showcase her eye-popping dancing abilities. She's done everything from performing silly Snapchat-inspired lip-sync renditions to intricately choreographed routines to singing while standing on her head and dressed as a Minion. Her goofiness, wide-ranging music tastes, and undeniable dance chops make her a perfect Musical.ly muse.

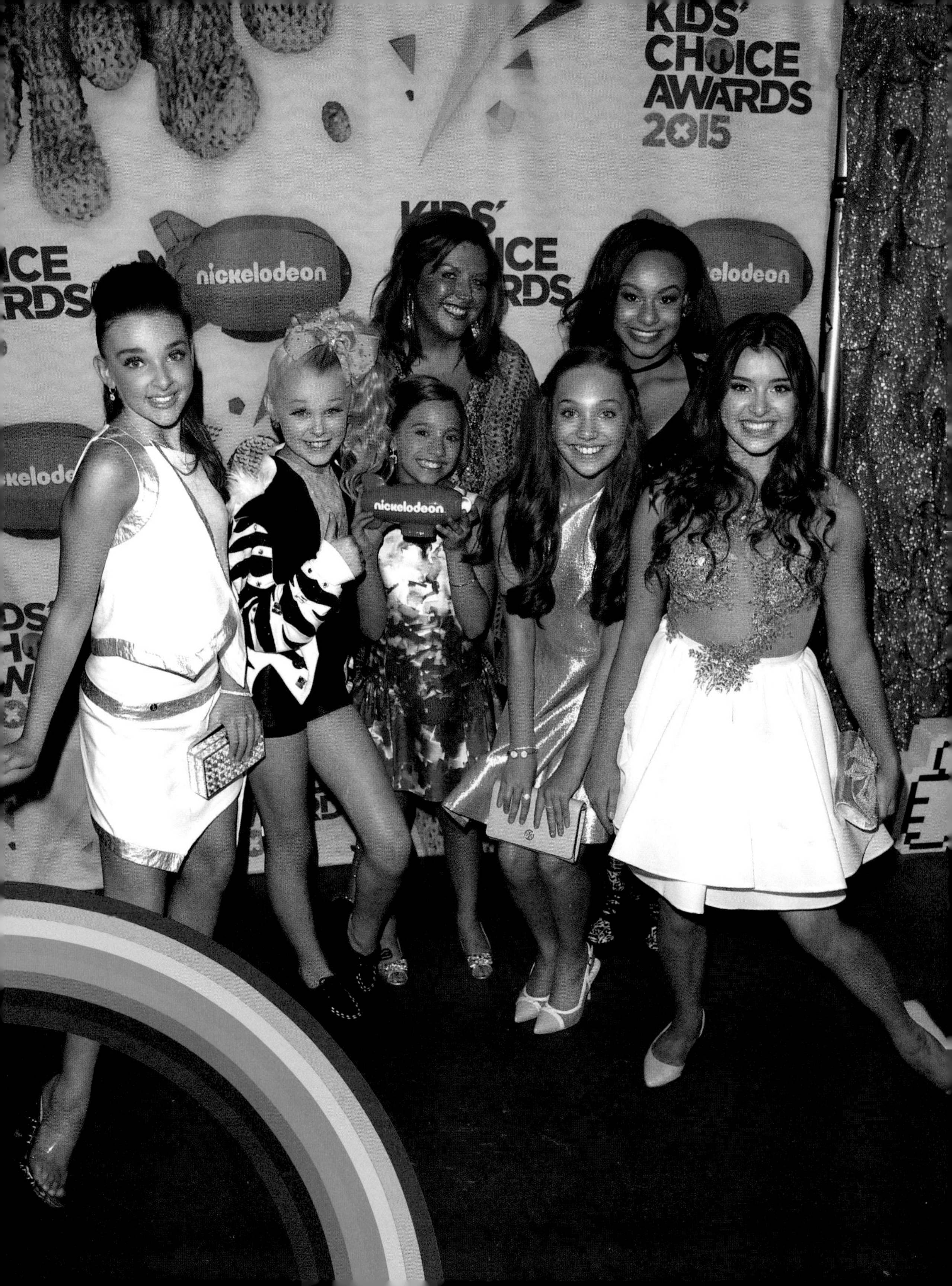
KIDS' CHOICE AWARDS 2015
nickelodeon

SHE THINKS MILLER IS ABBY-SOLUTELY FABULOUS!

JoJo got her big break as a featured dancer on *Abby's Ultimate Dance Competition* at age eight, and was a *Dance Moms* mainstay in seasons four through six. And while JoJo often clashed with the indomitable Abby Lee Miller, the two developed a deep mutual respect for one another. Aside from her mother, there is no individual who has been more influential on JoJo's career to this point.

Miller has faced adversity of late, including legal trouble and a battle with cancer, and JoJo has stood by her mentor through it all. After a visit to Miller in the hospital in May 2018, JoJo posted on Instagram, "Abby you have changed my life for forever [sic], I am so thankful for everything you have done for me (Table manners, how to survive in a plastic bubble, and more)! Thank you for letting us come by and visit you today! I love you. FOREVER. ♥ ☆"

"A lot of people my age try to act [older].... There's always time to grow older. You can never grow younger."

—To the *New York Times*

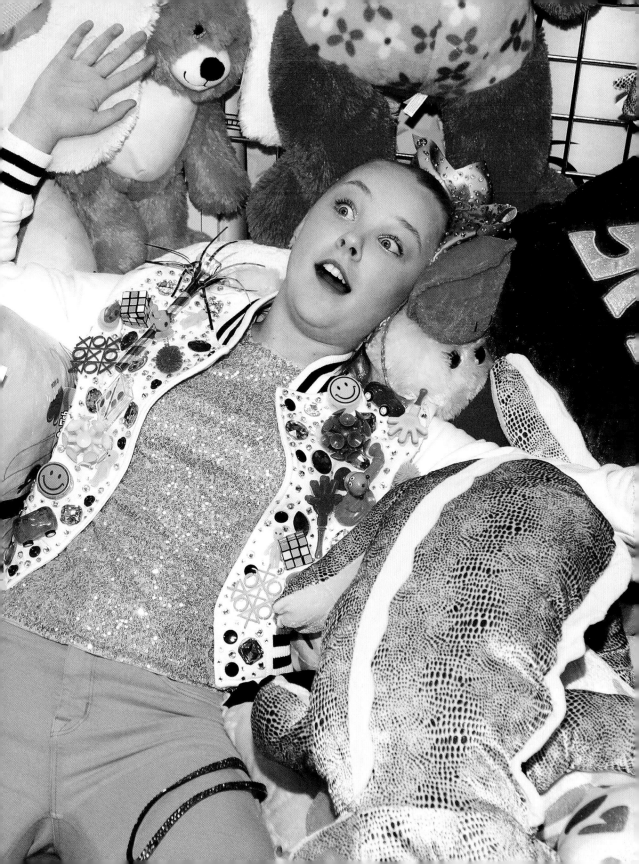

SHE CARES ABOUT GIVING BACK

JoJo is a strong anti-bullying advocate, and the people around the world who wear JoJo Bows make a powerful statement about empowerment. It's an issue to which JoJo remains fiercely devoted, but it's far from the only cause to which she's given her time and attention.

Inspired by her mentor and friend Abby Lee Miller's battle with cancer, JoJo recently presented Miller with a $10,000 check for Dancers Against Cancer. It's a cause JoJo has been involved with for years (she's pictured opposite attending a 2017 DAC benefit with guests). She has also represented the animal advocacy group the Lucy Pet Foundation and the T.J. Martell Foundation for cancer research, and she granted the wishes of young fans for the Make-A-Wish Foundation, among other very worthy causes.

12

SHE'S GOT JUICE

It started out as a simple idea. Every Wednesday JoJo would post a vlog and answer questions from her followers. The finale? Why, pouring juice all over herself, of course! *JoJo's Juice* started out as a daffy idea, but her 8 million-plus YouTube subscribers anxiously awaited each weekly post.

"The greatest thing about it is she literally was doing it all herself, from filming to editing to thumbnails to producing," Jessalynn told *USA Today*. "To see her have the success is really just the cherry on top."

Alas, all good things must come to an end. In February 2018 she announced that she was releasing her last *JoJo's Juice*. Still, followers can see original content from JoJo on her various channels and social media accounts—even YouTube. "It's my passion and I want to do it forever," she told Kidscreen.

13

SHE HAS A KNACK FOR LANGUAGES

JoJo certainly seems to have no trouble with words—the girl can talk a mile a minute. But did you know that she can also speak other languages? She picked up loads of Korean when her family hosted an exchange student in their home back in the day. (To this day, she gets excited when she's asked to speak in Korean.) But that's not all—she knows Spanish and Russian too. Is there anything she can't do?

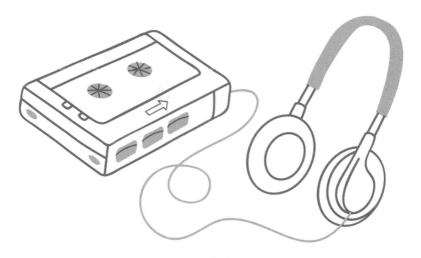

14

SHE KNOWS THE VALUE OF FRIENDSHIP

Watch her YouTube channel, her Instagram, or her music videos and you see it. JoJo's got squad goals, and one of them is surrounding herself with those people she cares about. True Siwanatorz can rattle off the names of her fellow *Dance Moms* crew, identify the pals in "Boomerang," (such as Kendall Vertes, opposite), and know Miranda Sings as well as they do JoJo. She credits her friends—from her hometown pals to fellow YouTubers to the cast and crew she hangs with on various sets—with keeping her sane in a crazy world.

And she remembers to always nurture those relationships. Her outlook is simple: "If you want really good friends, you've got to *be* a really good friend! Same goes for attracting good people in your life in the first place—if you put kindness out there, you're more likely to get it back," she advises in her autobiography. Words to live by.

15

SHE'S A SUCKER (GET IT?) FOR CANDY

It's only fitting that someone with as sweet and bubbly a personality as JoJo would be consumed by a candy obsession, right? Siwa's candy-coated fixation is next-level. The evidence? Well, she has a song called "Kid in a Candy Store," she has a signature nail and makeup line called Sweet Like Candy…heck, she even dresses like a rainbow-colored confection. Oh, and let's not forget that her autobiography, *JoJo's Guide to the Sweet Life*, is candy-themed, with each chapter named after a certain sweet treat.

16

SHE'S AN ADRENALINE JUNKIE!

Siwanatorz know how much energy JoJo has. But when she's not singing, dancing, acting, recording and cutting YouTube posts, or working on one of the many, many projects she has going, she takes time to relax…right? Far from it! Her idea of a relaxing afternoon is spending her time living dangerously.

"The one thing I love to do to just be a normal kid is going down to iFLY at Citywalk in Universal Studios," she told YayOMG.com. "It's amazing. It's indoor skydiving and it's the one semi-dangerous thing my mom will actually let me do."

17

SHE'S GOT PUPPY LOVE

JoJo grew up in a house filled with dogs. And to the Siwas, like many families, those pups are truly part of the family. JoJo has said often that at the end of a tough day, there's no better comfort than going home to her Yorkshire terrier, BowBow, for some unconditional love and snuggles (a cure-all, as many dog owners can attest).

But BowBow is no ordinary dog. Look no further than her Instagram page, @itsbowbowsiwa, to check out her glamorous life wearing crystal-studded hair bows and nibbling Chewy Vuiton bones! Besides being one of the best-dressed dogs in Hollywood, BowBow is also a celebrity in her own right. JoJo's book *JoJo Loves BowBow* chronicles a day in the life of the pampered pooch. The dog has her own video game avatar, a stuffed animal miniature, and as of the fall of 2018, her own animated series, *The JoJo and BowBow Show Show*.

SHE WANTS HER FANS TO STAND FOR SOMETHING

Siwanator is more than just a term for a fan of JoJo Siwa. It's a whole way of thinking. It's about how you treat others and, just as important, how you treat yourself.

"Being a Siwanator means being confident, positive, and supportive of others," JoJo writes in her autobiography. It's about being kind—even to the bullies. It's about knowing who you are and not compromising your own integrity. It's about embracing people's differences as well as their commonalities. It's a mind-set that resonates among Siwanatorz, and that love and support for one another is evident within their community. It's all about positivity. It's the unshakable bond that links JoJo's legion of fans.

SHE'S ANIMATED IN MORE WAYS THAN ONE

Sure, JoJo is bright and bubbly and hilarious—the very definition of animated. But did you know she also has a cartoon likeness? Nickelodeon's animated series *The JoJo and BowBow Show Show* follows the titular duo as they navigate the adventures of a world-famous pop star and her pampered pooch, from concert shenanigans to fashion shows to blisteringly jealous French poodles. JoJo (who else?) voices her own character on the show. And for anyone wondering if there's anything cuter than BowBow IRL, check out cartoon BowBow!

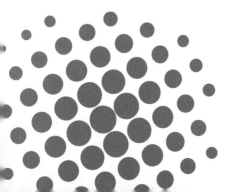

20

SHE'S HER DAD'S MINI-ME

A lot of people assume JoJo is a carbon copy of her mom, especially because the two of them have been linked in the spotlight for so long. But it's actually her dad, Tom, with whom she most closely identifies. "My dad and me, we're two peas in a pod," she writes in her memoir. "It's a good thing we have my brother and my mom to keep us grounded!"

According to JoJo, she and her dad are the ones who can't sit still. She gets her energy, her competitive spirit, her tenacity, and her sense of humor from her dad. They're also more likely to have their heads in the clouds. Luckily there's balance in the Siwa household; Jessalynn and Jayden are calm and steady.

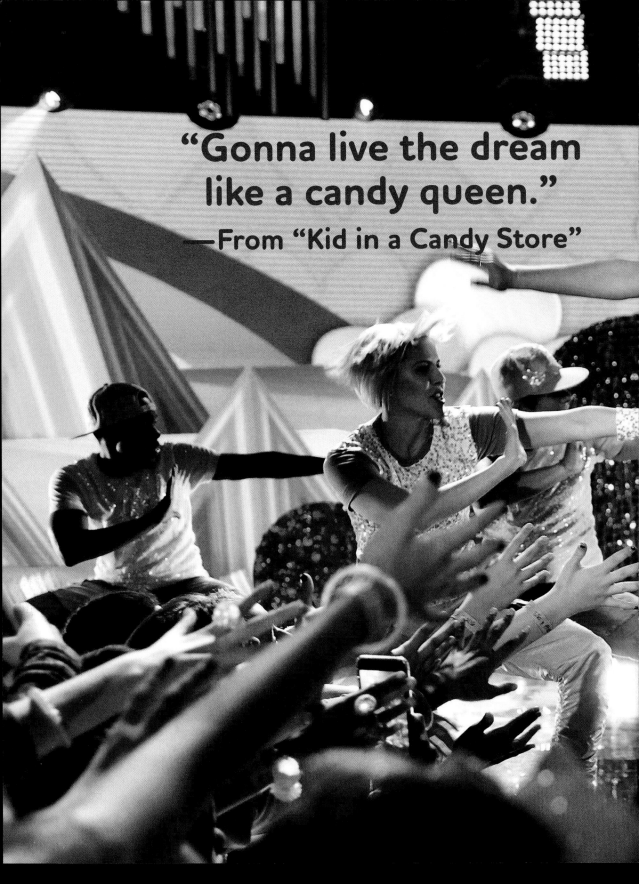

"Gonna live the dream
like a candy queen."
—From "Kid in a Candy Store"

SHE'S A NATURAL BRUNETTE

Ask anyone, and they'll tell you that JoJo is real. As the star explained on her YouTube channel, "A lot of people think like 'JoJo' is fake or 'JoJo' is a character. But...you guys know me—this is how I always am."

Still, there's one thing about JoJo that isn't real: her hair color! It turns out that Jessalynn started bleaching JoJo's hair when she was a young competitive dancer. Ultimately, the flowing blond ponytail has become part of JoJo's signature look.

Curious what she looks like with dark hair? Check out her Instagram for a pic of a certain pint-sized brunette!

22

SHE HAS HER OWN VIDEO GAME LIKENESS

Fans of JoJo can see her vlogs on her YouTube channel, connect with her via social media, or just tune in to Nickelodeon. And now that JoJo has been added to *Star Stable*, they can also interact with her avatar online. The game, which boasts players from 182 countries worldwide, is a multiplayer problem-solving and adventure game in which players explore the fictional world of Jorvik on horseback—leaving time to take brief stops at the disco to dance with their favorite bow-bedecked pop star, of course!

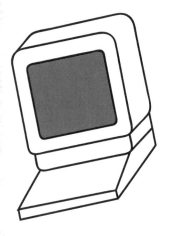

SHE LOVES
A GOOD HASHTAG

Like any good Instagrammer and Twitterer, she's aces when it comes to crafting hashtags. She's got it all covered, from silly (#icanmakeyoudance, #bowsmakeeverythingbetter) to inspirational (#dreamcrazybig, #girlsneverquit). She even added a hashtag to her autobiography title: #peaceouthaterz!

Most important, she's getting the word out about what really matters to her: putting a stop to bullying. Fans are picking up on JoJo's positive vibes, spreading #bestiesnotbullies and #beyourselfie the world wide!

SHE TAKES BEING A ROLE MODEL SERIOUSLY

Long ago, after a bullying experience of her own, JoJo made a conscious choice to use her social media for good above all else. And she has made good on that promise to herself, creating a community of loving, supportive Siwanatorz and blocking out the haters.

She's also aware that all eyes are on her, and she holds herself to a high standard. After fellow YouTuber Jake Paul was criticized for showing content many felt was disturbing for his young fans, JoJo posted this pledge to her followers: "I promise you forever that my content will always be family friendly and safe for your kids. It is hard to trust what's on the internet but I can tell you that I know my responsibilities, and I will never put anything online that is inappropriate or not safe for children to watch."

It's one of the main reasons why so many parents love JoJo; she sets a great example for her young fans.

SHE'S GOT STYLE TO SHARE

Remember that killer appliquéd bomber jacket that she wore to her fourteenth birthday bash? You know, the silver one with the cupcakes and the unicorns and the bows? Well, that jacket, plus a number of other sparkly, sweet, and adorbs pieces that JoJo has worn over the years, have been mass-produced so that you too can wear them. JoJo's Closet launched at Target stores in 2017, but numerous other retailers carry JoJo apparel too. No Target near you? Try Walmart, Kohl's, JCPenney, Justice, Sears, Claire's Accessories, Party City, Amazon, or basically any retailer for JoJo merch! And stay tuned to her social media accounts; she'll keep you posted on where to look next!

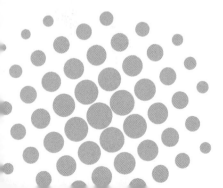

SHE CAN PLAY THE PIANO

JoJo can sing, dance, act…she's a director, producer, and YouTube influencer…she's a business mogul and a role model…she's a whirling dervish of energy and creativity. And yes, she can play music too.

YouTube followers have watched her evolution unfold as she's become a more assured pianist, beginning with simple ditties and ultimately playing renditions of her favorite songs, including a beautiful version of Snow Patrol's "Chasing Cars." You can also see her chops on full display in the music video for "Only Getting Better," in which she plays the piano as only she can—on a red piano glittering with rhinestones.

SHE AND HER BRO ARE TIGHTER THAN TIGHT

They're almost three years apart (2 years and 364 days, to be exact), but they've always been "crazy close." Followers of JoJo on social media know Jayden well, as he frequently appeared in her *JoJo's Juice* offerings as well as on her other accounts. (For a good laugh, check out their hilarious send-up of James Corden's "Carpool Karaoke" on JoJo's YouTube channel.)

They clearly have *tons* of fun whenever they're together—swimming, playing video games, playing baseball, and especially playing pranks. It's also clear that they are each other's biggest fans. "He's the most unconditionally loving brother ever," she writes in her autobiography.

And now that her dad and brother have relocated to L.A. from Nebraska, don't be surprised if you see Jayden's face popping up on the small screen sometime soon!

28

SHE TURNED HER GIFT OF GAB INTO A GIG

In October 2017 JoJo added a new feather in her cap when she became cohost of Nickelodeon's *Lip Sync Battle Shorties*, a kid-oriented spin-off of the original *Lip Sync Battle* game show. It's a showcase for young and talented kiddos, and it's mad fun. JoJo's energy and sparkle are on full display, and her goofiness makes her a perfect complement to cohost Nick Cannon.

And while hosting duties might not be the most obvious role for JoJo, it's actually an opportunity for her to use one of her strongest personality traits. "I've always been able to carry on a conversation with anyone—it's a skill I'm really proud of," she writes in her autobiography. And it shows!

29

SHE'S A TALL DRINK OF WATER

On-screen, JoJo is larger than life. And in real life, standing with a dancer's poise at 5'9", she's far from a giant, but you never would have guessed it from people's reactions when she recently revealed her height in a YouTube vlog. The Internet. Lost. Its. Mind. Haters and supporters alike marveled that she was the same height as celebs from Justin Bieber to Tom Hardy to Serena Williams.

"I've just been tall my whole life so it doesn't faze me, but it fazes some of you guys," she said of the reactions. Just more proof positive that she's comfortable in her own skin.

SHE'S HAD
A FEW BREAKS

Perhaps it's bound to happen to someone as physically active and adventure-seeking as JoJo, but the girl seems to have suffered her fair share of injuries—especially when it comes to breaking her smallest digit.

She was eight when it happened the first time, during the very unlikely scenario of playing dodgeball with a giant sumo wrestler on the trampoline. (Wait, now that it's on paper, that does sound a little risky.) An injury to the same pinkie effectively ended her fast-pitch softball career.

Luckily, she's also a good field doctor—she did some quick thinking and created a makeshift brace by taping her pinkie to a popsicle stick!

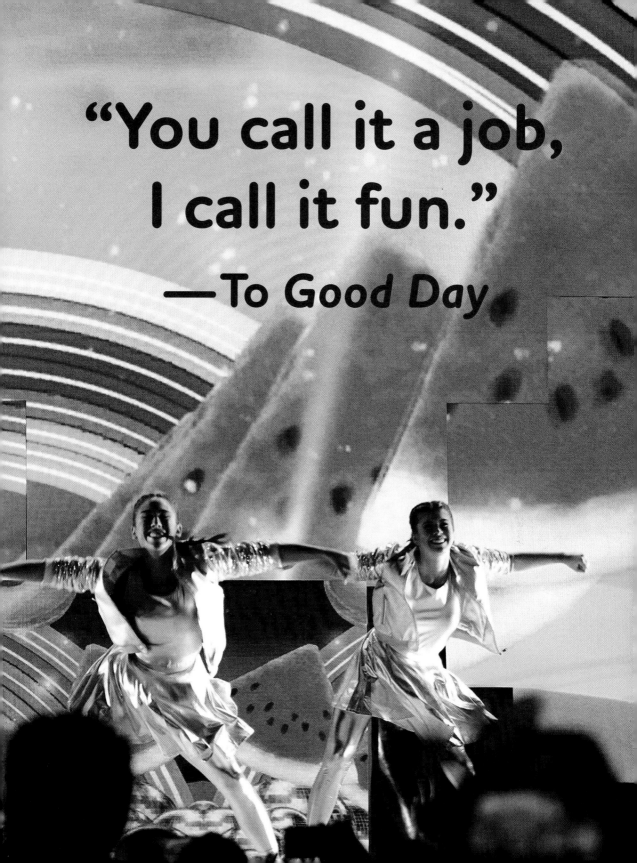

"You call it a job, I call it fun."
—To Good Day

SHE'S PART OF THE NICK FAMILY

When JoJo signed a deal with Nickelodeon in March 2017 to become the newest member of the Nickelodeon family, Shelly Sumpter Gillyard, executive VP of talent, music, and events at Nickelodeon, spoke enthusiastically of the pairing: "JoJo's an entrepreneur, her family is everything to her, and she is happy just being a kid."

Since then, JoJo has appeared in numerous Nick programs—cohosting *Lip Sync Battle Shorties*, guest-starring on *School of Rock*, and appearing in Nick's *Sizzling Summer Camp Special*. Nick also did a documentary called *JoJo Siwa: My World*, which gives fans an insider's look at JoJo's crazy life.

As she writes in her autobiography, "All the Nick friends are like a big family." Suffice it to say, so far she's having the *slime* of her life!

32

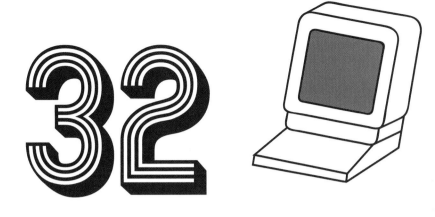

SHE OBSESSES OVER *GREY MATTER*

In those rare hours when she's not rehearsing, cutting videos, acting, or otherwise working herself to the point of exhaustion, JoJo makes time to unwind like the rest of us. And her happiest guilty pleasure? The McDreamiest and McSteamiest primetime soap of them all: *Grey's Anatomy*.

"When it comes down to it, I am 100 percent the number one fan of *Grey's Anatomy*," she said on YouTube. Proof positive that JoJo does everything with maximum effort and dedication? She's binge-watched the previous thirteen seasons in the span of two years. She even had a pair of *Grey's*-style scrubs made, complete with a Grey Sloan Memorial Hospital badge with her name on it. Now *that's* fan commitment!

SHE'S AN INSANELY HARD WORKER

JoJo was born in Omaha, Nebraska, far from the bright lights of Hollywood. But from the earliest age she can remember, she wanted to be a star. She started dancing competitively at age two. She also starred in her first television commercial—a spot for hardwood floors—when she was still in diapers. Come what may, she was headed for the spotlight. "I always wanted more," she said in her TED Talk. And she has met every goal that she's set for herself, knocking them down like a row of dominoes.

"She's the hardest-working person of [her age]....that I've ever met," said Jace Norman (opposite), her costar on the movie *Blurt*. And so far, all that hard work is paying off. From her on-screen success to her merchandising empire, JoJo is on fire. Now it's on to the next goal. Pop stardom can't be far behind.

34

SHE'S WARY OF THE GREEN-EYED MONSTER

JoJo promotes positivity in all realms, and one of the things that upsets her the most is when people tear other people down to build themselves up. Sometimes it's just not your day, and when it's someone else's turn to get something good, you should be happy for them, not jealous. Jealousy is pointless, she says!

"My mom and I always say, 'Life is like an upside-down pyramid—there's room for everyone at the top,'" she writes in her autobiography. And true to her word, you'll see her practicing what she preaches—she's constantly dishing out encouragement and congratulations to her friends and peers for their accomplishments.

35

SHE LEARNED MORE THAN STEPS ON *DANCE MOMS*

The reality show *Dance Moms* certainly had its share of drama, but amid the grueling practices and harsh criticisms of Abby Lee Miller, alumna JoJo took with her a host of life lessons. "[Abby] taught me how to sink or swim," she told *People*. "Another [piece of] advice she gave me is you've got to be able to put your heart out on a platter and be ready for someone to stab it. That has happened a few times too!"

Above all, she learned about forging friendships despite being competitive. Speaking of her fellow dancers (including, opposite, Kendall Vertes, Brynn Rumfallo, and Kalani Hilliker), she continued, "We'll be forever sisters."

36

SHE'S BEEN
ALL DOLLED UP

It's not every pop star who can boast a doll version of herself. In JoJo's case, she has not one but *several* mini-mes. From big to small, talking to poseable, she seems to have doppelgangers in every store. The dolls come in an array of rainbow-splashed and unicorn-clad fashions, just like JoJo herself. And what's a doll without a canine accessory? Don't worry—BowBow's in on the action too.

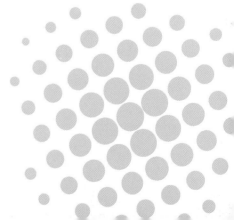

37

SHE'S A (BEST-SELLING!) BOOK AUTHOR

Time to add another hyphen (as in, she's a multi-multi-hyphenate). In 2018 the dancer-singer-actress-vlogger-host became a bona fide book author with the release of *JoJo's Guide to the Sweet Life*, her inspirational autobiography about her life so far. The book tackles everything from advice on dealing with bullies to how to go after your dreams, big and small.

The release joins a line of activity and sticker books, journals, and craft books aimed at Siwanatorz. Not enough for you? Wonder puppy BowBow has gotten in on the action too, with JoJo releasing his paw-tobiographical *JoJo Loves BowBow: A Day in the Life of the World's Cutest Canine*.

38

SHE'S GOT A HIDDEN SECRET

Her trademark bow and side ponytail are instantly recognizable, but there's something you might not know about JoJo's famous hairstyle. Underneath that bow are not one but four ponytail elastics corralling her 'do. And it's not just any ponytail holders that'll do—she uses one hot pink, one neon green, one yellow, and one bright orange to do the job. It's a routine that dates back to her thirteenth birthday, and she hasn't missed a single day since.

39

SHE'S LOYAL TO HER BESTIES

They're in her music videos, they're in her vlogs...everywhere you look, you see JoJo's squad. There are her hometown homies, her *Dance Mom* peeps, her circle of friends in Cali. And then, of course, there's her BFF Colleen Ballinger (opposite), super-famous YouTuber and creator of Miranda Sings. "Miranda and I are best friends, but she doesn't want anyone besides us to know that," JoJo joked. "But Miranda is a character who is played by Colleen Ballinger who in real life is my best friend," JoJo told the *Sydney Morning Herald*. "Colleen is so talented and the way her creativity comes to life in the Miranda character is amazing," she gushed.

Surrounding herself with people she loves and celebrating their accomplishments is the cornerstone of JoJo's approach to friendship. As she writes in her autobiography, "There's room for everyone to do great things."

40

SHE DOESN'T LIKE *WHAT*?!

She's about as wholesome American as they come. But despite growing up in America's heartland, there's one thing that JoJo isn't down with: American food. Hot dogs, hamburgers, french fries… she doesn't care for any of it. She doesn't even really go in for the world-class steaks that make her hometown famous! Lest anyone think she's subsisting on candy alone (as her songs and wardrobe might suggest), there is room in her heart for comfort food. She just throws in for pizza rolls and ramen instead. (And yes, she usually eats sensibly; salad and salmon are her favorite foods.)

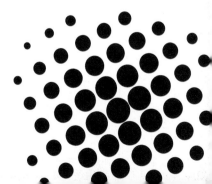

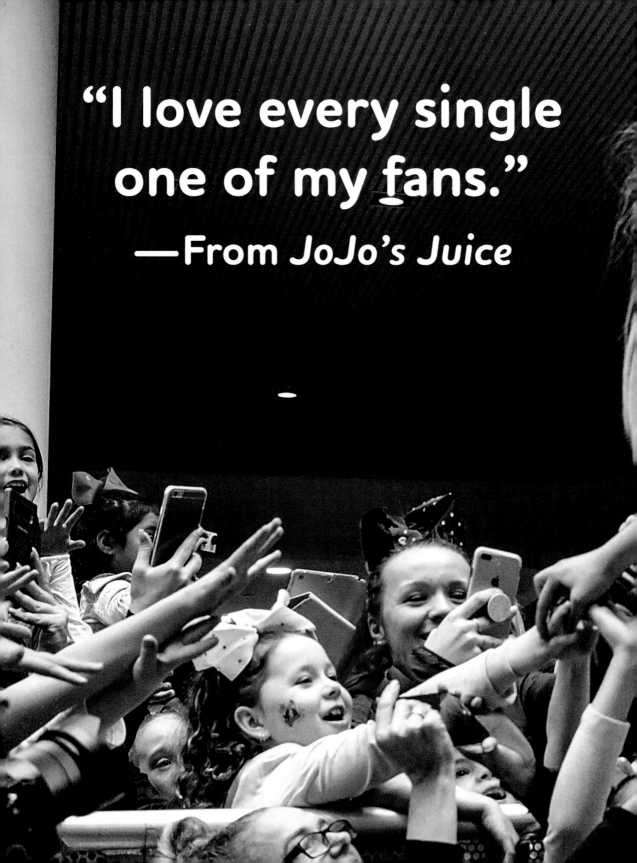

"I love every single one of my fans."

—From *JoJo's Juice*

41

SHE'S IN GOOD COMPANY

JoJo's not the only star to hail from Nebraska's biggest city. Omaha is the hometown of everyone from Hollywood royalty such as Marlon Brando and the Fonda family to political titans such as former US president Gerald Ford and civil rights activist Malcolm X. "The Oracle of Omaha," billionaire Warren Buffett, calls Omaha home. Musicians including Bright Eyes' Conor Oberst, singer-songwriter Elliott Smith, and the band 311 all hail from Omaha. It's spawned funny people too—such as *Workaholics'* Adam Devine and filmmaker Alexander Payne, just to name a couple. And is it any coincidence that arguably the most famous dancer of all time, Fred Astaire, was an Omahan?

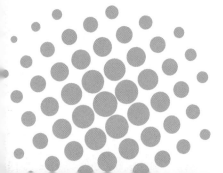

Greetings from OMAHA NEBRASKA

42

SHE'S GOT
MERCH FOR DAYS

If you haven't noticed by now, there's a whole JoJo Siwa empire out there. Siwanatorz can nab everything from bedding to party supplies to slime-making kits to beach towels to king-size plush cupcakes and unicorns and beyond. Looking to doll yourself up like JoJo? Check out her line of makeup and nail-art kits. Want to sing along to your favorite JoJo songs? Grab the karaoke machine or the JoJo microphone or perform with your singing doll. How about rocking that JoJo style in the classroom? There are oodles of school supplies just for you! You want to kick it in her kicks? She's got a variety of sequined high-tops with, yes, bows. You can even craft your own DIY hair bows with her Cool Maker bow maker. Chances are, if you can think of it, it's probably out there!

43

SHE'S ALL ABOUT THE BOW BOWS

It's a fashion statement with deep roots. ("I've been wearing bows for my whole, entire life—since I was in preschool and obviously now and above and beyond," JoJo told *Ad Age*.) But her JoJo Bows are far more than a style choice—they're a symbol.

The bows are an extension of her campaign against bullies, an outward message that the wearer won't tolerate the hate. And Siwanatorz who wear her bows, according to JoJo via her Instagram, project the following virtues:

1. You're confident, you believe in yourself and others
2. You say no to bullying and other people can look at us and know that we're kind and will be their friend
3. You like to have fun, stand out, and are NEVER afraid to be different

JoJo's positive message has spread like wildfire, as kids around the world have been buying the JoJo Bows en masse. (She sold 25 *million* bows in 2017!) Because what's more in fashion than kindness?

44

SHE'S A UNICORN AT HER CORE

She's unique. She's fun. She's special. Some might say…magical. It's easy to see why JoJo identifies with the unicorn as her spirit animal. "I'm bright, I'm sparkly, fun, crazy, and creative," she told Sweety High by way of explanation.

And the girl is *unicorn-obsessed*, to put it lightly. The world's most magical mythical creature can be seen on dozens of JoJo's outfits, from fuzzy onesies to full-body unicorn costumes to the appliqués she wears on her shoes and clothes. It's a popular motif in her merch too. She even sells a JoJo-branded stuffed unicorn plushie!

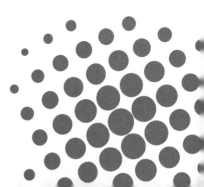

SHE FOLLOWS THE GRANDMA RULE

It's a great thing to consider when you're faced with a choice: *What would grandma say?* Inspired by her brother, Jayden ("the perfect kid," she writes in her autobiography), JoJo finds the rule—and his example—helps her keep her bearings.

As she explains on her YouTube vlog "The Most Important Rule," "If you wouldn't do it in front of your grandma, if you wouldn't say it in front of your grandma, if you wouldn't act like it in front of your grandma, you should not be doing it, saying it, acting like it."

And since JoJo values kindness over all other virtues, Grandma must be proud indeed.

46

SHE'S A STRAIGHT-UP JOCK

Obviously JoJo is a born dancer. And you don't have to be a *Dance Moms* watcher to know how much coordination, athleticism, and skill go into being a serious dancer. But that's not the only sport JoJo enjoys. Back in Nebraska, she played catcher and right fielder (she had an arm!) on a competitive softball team. She also competed in tumbling, gymnastics, and cheerleading before turning her focus solely to dance once more.

These days, you're likely to find her playing pickup games of basketball or football in her free time—what little of it there is!

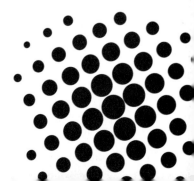

47

SHE'S A SNEAKERHEAD

It should come as no surprise that the girl who sings an ode to high top shoes has dozens upon dozens of them. "I'm obsessed with shoes," she admits on her vlog. Among the brands she favors? Converse, Puma, Nike, Adidas, and Vlado. Astute JoJo watchers have no doubt spotted her killer kicks—rhinestone-bedazzled Chuck Taylors, studded sneakers, footwear with exaggerated bows...even custom designer creations like the slime-themed Gucci sneakers, opposite. She even has "pie top" shoes that order pizzas directly from Pizza Hut. Now *that's* commitment!

It serves to follow that she's passed on her shoe obsession to her fans, who can now have JoJo-inspired sneakers of their own. Because bows (and rhinestones and sequins and studs) make everything better!

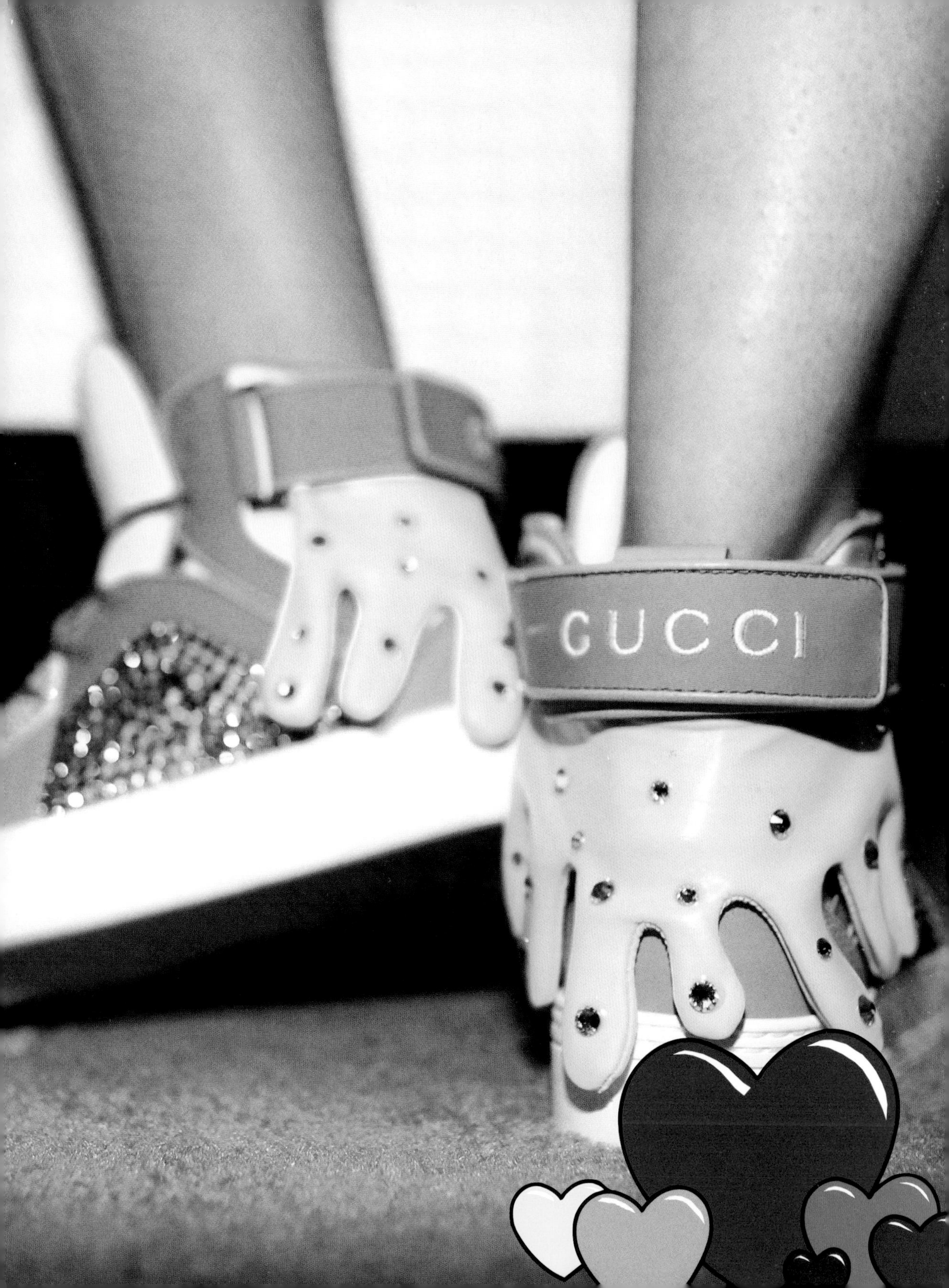
CUCCI

SHE'S BIG DOWN UNDER

Besides being a megastar in North America, she's also got a huge following overseas! On a recent trip to Australia, she was overwhelmed by crowds everywhere she went—an estimated 15,000 fans turned up to a free show in Melbourne (five times the capacity of the venue), some families camping out overnight just to get a glimpse of her. She's a familiar face on Australia's Nickelodeon, which rolled out *JoJo's 5 Days Down Under* when the singer hit its shores. She's also a big hit in the UK, where JoJo Bows have swept classrooms everywhere.

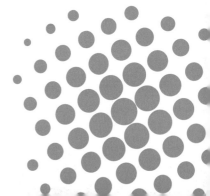

49

SHE'S GOT A KILLER SQUAD

No diva makes it to the top without help, and JoJo is no exception. She's surrounded by an amazing group of people who help her to look and be her best every day ("Love my team so much," she Instagrammed). Wonder who's behind all those great dance moves? Well, a lot of them are the work of Guy Amir, otherwise known as Guy Groove. JoJo's signature 'do and makeup are the responsibility of Diana Kaz, keeper of the rainbow extensions and, of course, the multitude of bows. Arturo Chavez designs a ton of the wild and sparkly clothes that have become a JoJo staple. Publicist Kimber Hamill-Garten gets the word out. And "the best manager in the world" Caryn Sterling gets things done. And of course all roads to JoJo lead through her mom, Jessalynn, whom JoJo calls her best friend and biggest supporter. Those are just a few of the many people behind the scenes in JoJo's world.

SHE'S ONLY GETTING BETTER

JoJo's quest for world domination seems to be all but assured at this point. And it's come with a lot of grit and determination. Fans, afforded an insider's look at their idol's life, know all too well how much JoJo has put into her career. She brings her dancer's work ethic to everything she does, whether it's cutting videos, learning instruments and songwriting, acting, voice training, marketing, and beyond.

The fifteen-year-old dynamo, who fellow YouTuber Shane Dawson described as "one of the smartest people I've ever met," is also one of Hollywood's hardest workers. And to quote her own lyrics, "it's only getting better."